Here's What I Need You To Know

I AM AUTISM

Written by Jeremiah Josey
and Simone Greggs

Illustrated By: Hilbert Bermejo

Rev. date: 07/10/2013

To order additional copies of this book, contact:
Xlibris Corporation
1-888-795-4274
www.Xlibris.com
Orders@Xlibris.com

To my legacy,

Maya and Jeremiah

One in fifty children in the
United States have Autism.

HERE'S WHAT I WANT YOU TO KNOW...

That I want you to accept me for
Who I am and all I strive to be
God made me this way

HERE'S WHAT I WANT YOU TO KNOW...

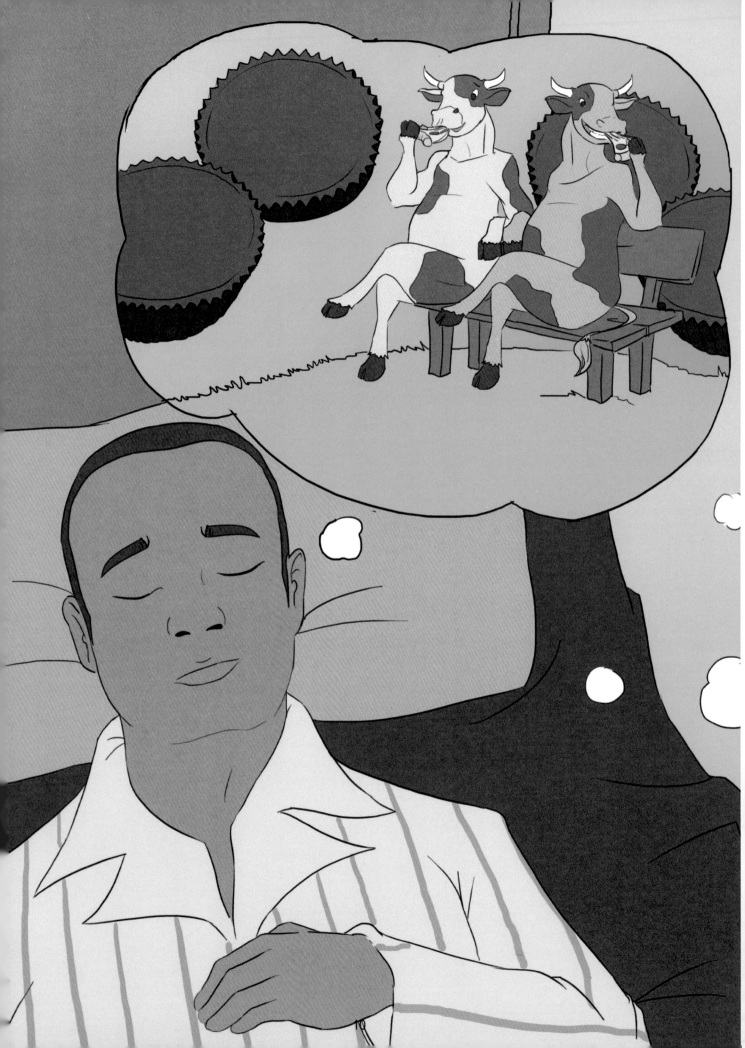

That my mom loves
me beyond my
wildest dreams
challenges and
extremes.

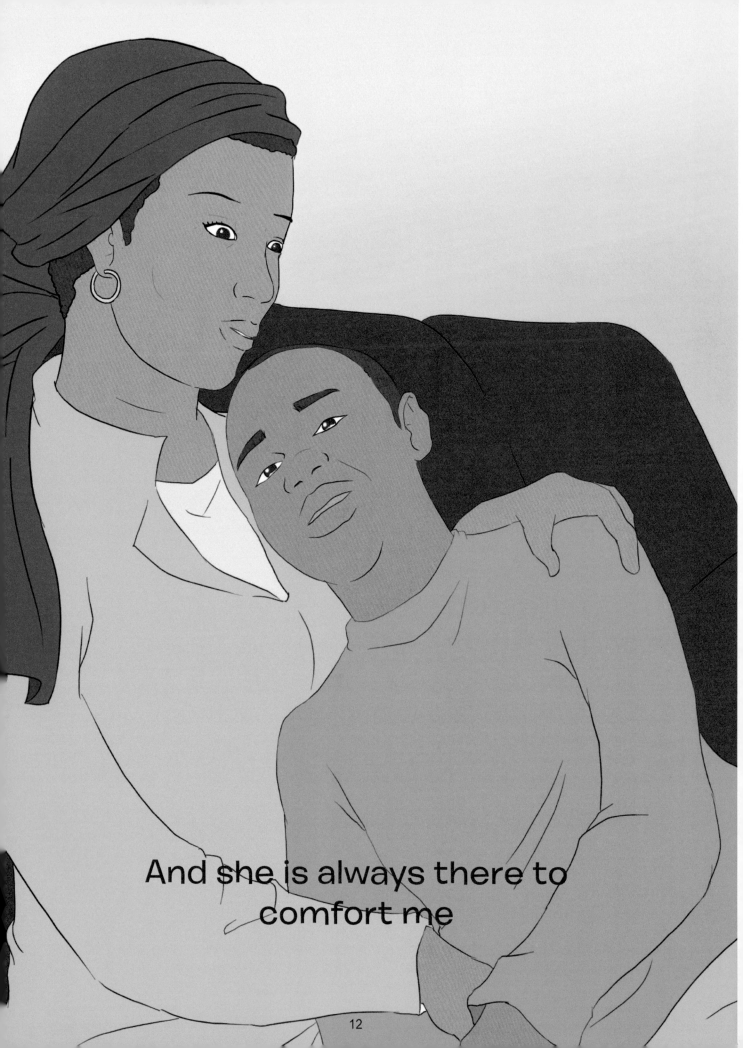

And she is always there to comfort me

HERE'S WHAT I WANT YOU TO KNOW...

I AM AUTISM I AM AUTISM I AM AUTISM
I AM AUTISM I AM AUTISM I AM AUTISM
I AM AUTISM I AM AUTISM I AM AUTISM
I AM AUTISM I AM AUTISM I AM AUTISM
I AM AUTISM I AM AUTISM I AM AUTISM
I AM AUTISM I AM AUTISM I AM AUTISM
I AM AUTISM I AM AUTISM I AM AUTISM
I AM AUTISM I AM AUTISM I AM AUTISM
I AM AUTISM I AM AUTISM I AM AUTISM
I AM AUTISM I AM AUTISM I AM AUTISM
I AM AUTISM I AM AUTISM I AM AUTISM
I AM AUTISM I AM AUTISM I AM AUTISM
I AM AUTISM I AM AUTISM I AM AUTISM
I AM AUTISM I AM AUTISM I AM AUTISM
I AM AUTISM I AM AUTISM I AM AUTISM
I AM AUTISM I AM AUTISM I AM AUTISM
I AM AUTISM I AM AUTISM I AM AUTISM
I AM AUTISM I AM AUTISM I AM AUTISM

I LOVE
TO RECITE
WORDS
OVER
AND OVER

Get loud in a crowd
Make silly noises
But I know how to turn it down
I refocus
Sometimes all I wish I had to say was

HERE'S WHAT I WANT YOU TO KNOW...

$$\frac{a}{b} \div \frac{c}{d} = \frac{a}{b} \times \frac{d}{c} =$$

Math problems are like scrambled
eggs in my head
But I'm sure Albert Einstein
had thoughts
Dancing in his head!

HERE'S WHAT I WANT YOU TO KNOW...

I desire friends because
Friends are precious like diamonds
and jewels
So why can't you stop treating me
like a fool!

HERE'S WHAT I WANT YOU TO KNOW...

When I feel lonely and empty inside
Can't this void be filled sometimes?
Don't be afraid
Just give me a chance

'Cause even the most brilliant
minds explore

HERE'S WHAT I WANT YOU TO KNOW...

That my heart beats like Yours

A portion of the proceeds from this book
will be donated to
All The Love Inc.

All the love means lending a helping hand and caring for special people. Jeremiah

The purpose of All The Love Inc. is to raise awareness about autism and the importance of early detection in the African American, Hispanic, and other minority groups. All The Love Inc. seeks to provide grants to families caring for children with autism.

Be sure to visit our website,
www.AlltheLoveInc.com.

www.facebook.com/loveforjeremiah

Twitter: @GreggsSimone

83784249R00020

Made in the USA
San Bernardino, CA
30 July 2018